DRAW

MONSTERS

A Step-by-Step Guide

by
Damon J. Reinagle

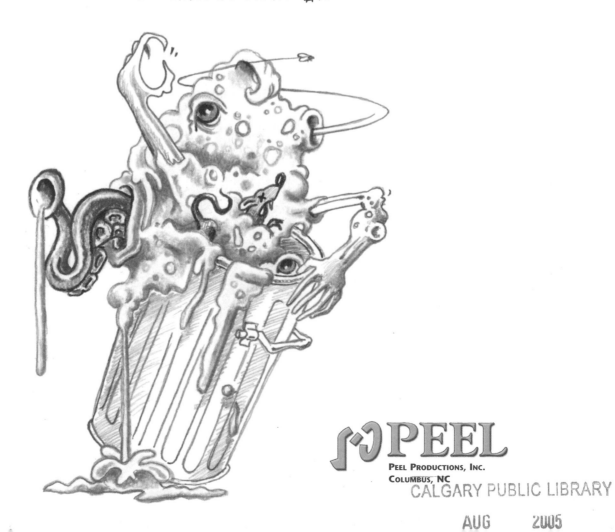

PEEL PRODUCTIONS, INC.
COLUMBUS, NC

AUG   2005

Printed in China

Library of Congress Cataloging-in-Publication Data
Reinagle, Damon J.
   Draw Monsters : a step-by-step guide / Damon J.
Reinagle.
         p. cm.
      ISBN 0-939217-34-1 (sewn paper binding : alk. paper)
1. Monsters in art--Juvenile literature. 2. Drawing--
Technique--Juvenile literature. I. Title: Draw monsters.
II. Title.

NC1764.8.M65R45 2005

743'.87--dc22

2004019792

**Distributed to the trade and art
markers in North and South
America by**

NORTH LIGHT BOOKS,

**an imprint of F&W Publications,
Inc.**
**4700 East Galbraith Road
Cincinnati, OH 45236**

(800) 289-0963

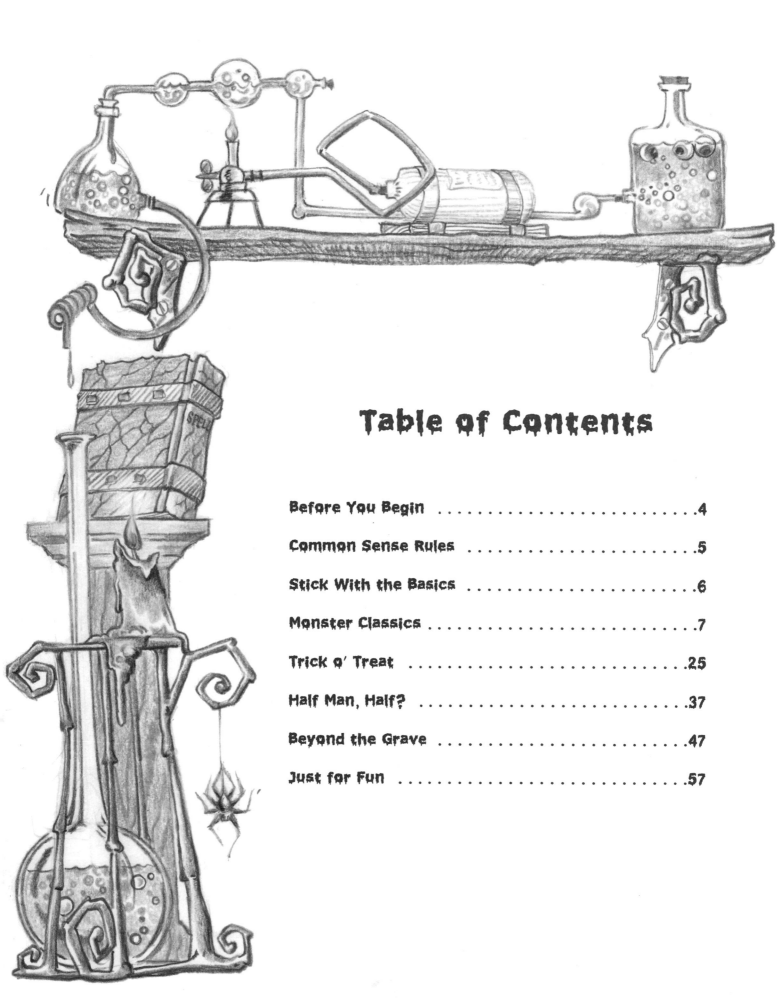

Table of Contents

Before You Begin 4

Common Sense Rules .5

Stick With the Basics .6

Monster Classics 7

Trick o' Treat 25

Half Man, Half? 37

Beyond the Grave 47

Just for Fun 57

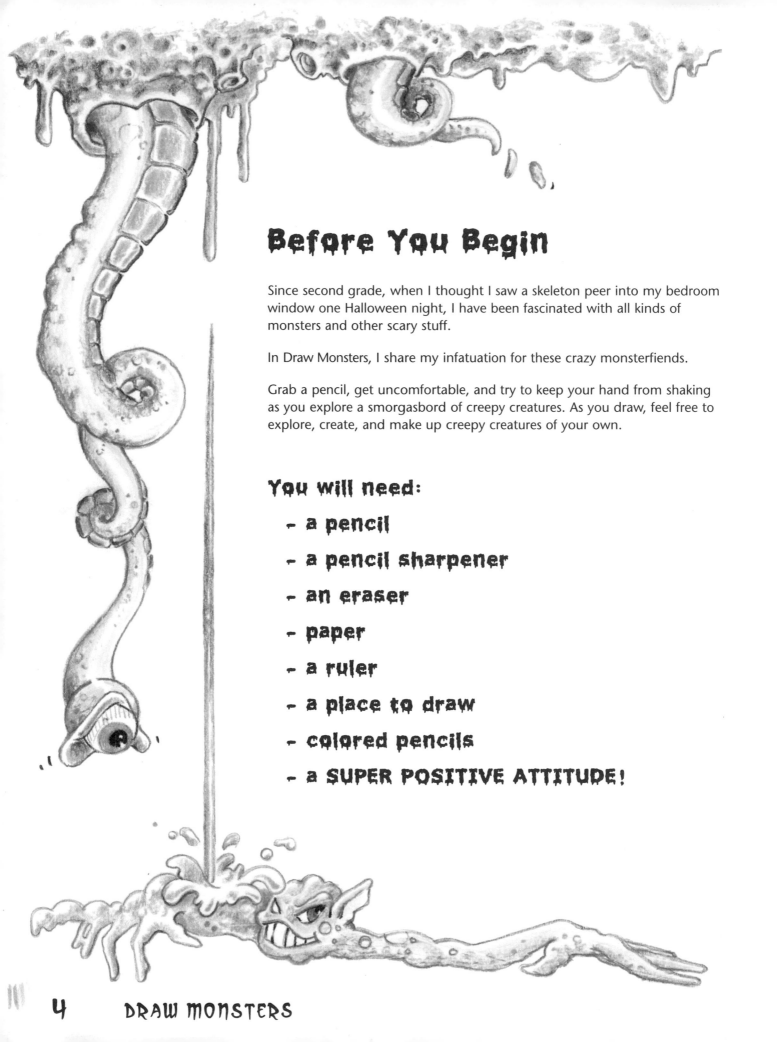

Before You Begin

Since second grade, when I thought I saw a skeleton peer into my bedroom window one Halloween night, I have been fascinated with all kinds of monsters and other scary stuff.

In Draw Monsters, I share my infatuation for these crazy monsterfiends.

Grab a pencil, get uncomfortable, and try to keep your hand from shaking as you explore a smorgasbord of creepy creatures. As you draw, feel free to explore, create, and make up creepy creatures of your own.

You will need:

- a pencil
- a pencil sharpener
- an eraser
- paper
- a ruler
- a place to draw
- colored pencils
- a SUPER POSITIVE ATTITUDE!

Common Sense Rules

Rule 1 Look! See the shapes!

Whether you are drawing a monster or a sack of potatoes, the main thing is to see the shapes. Simple circles, squares, rectangles, and triangles form the basis of our visual world.

Rule 2 Always sketch super lightly!

Use light sketch lines as guidelines to begin and build up your drawings. Erasing lines is much easier to do if you sketch lightly at first.

Rule 3 Be creative!

You can quickly become a good artist by following the step-by-step drawings in this book. The real adventure in drawing comes when you make up your own characters and your own imaginary worlds. Go for it! Use your imagination!

Rule 4 Practice, practice, practice!

Dr. Frankenstein didn't succeed with his first attempt at monster making. It took him many tries. Practice, practice, practice, and you will succeed!

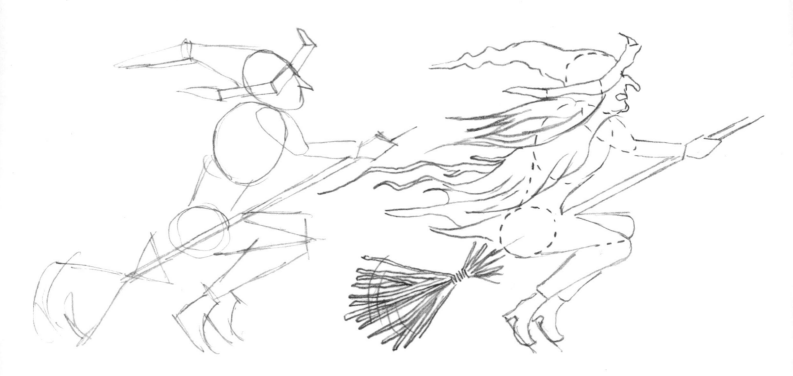

Stick With the Basics

Almost all of the figures in this book begin with oval shaped heads. The bodies of the figures are drawn with basic shapes: circles, ovals, rectangles, and triangles. Arms and legs often begin as lines (rods) and ovals or circles (joints) to help you envision the position and proportion. Remember, stick with basic shapes to begin your drawing and you can't go wrong! Complicated drawings can be created when you start with simple, basic shapes.

The Mad Scientist

Whenever there's a new creature to be made, the mad scientist is around. Count on this nutty professor to drop the brain, er... ball because after all, he is the Mad Scientist!

1 Lightly sketch an oval head. Draw a diagonal line to begin his shoulders. Draw a V-shaped neckline.

2 Look at the shape of his lab coat. Draw it.

3 Starting at the top, add two curved lines to start his wild hairdo. Draw circles to begin his glasses and add a second V-shaped neck line. Draw two lines down the front of his coat. Look at the lines (rods), oval and square (joints) used to begin his arm. Lightly sketch these.

4 Starting at the top, lightly sketch the lines (rods) and oval (joints) for the second arm. Sketch a large oval to begin the brain he's holding. Add more hair lines. Draw the nose and mouth. Add lines to make his lab coat longer. Add additional lines to shape his left arm. Using simple lines, make a beaker.

5 Look closely at his raised right arm. Draw the brain, hand, and arm lines you see. Add more hair and finish his moustache. Note the position of his legs and feet. Using lines (rods) and ovals (joints), sketch the bone structure. Add lines to shape his jacket and pants.

6 Look at the final drawing. Erase extra sketch lines. Add details you see. Darken the final lines. Add color.

As the Mad Scientist says, "With a good brain you can do anything!"

Igor

Every mad scientist needs an able bodied assistant, one with sure hands and good looks! Igor fits the bill.

1 Look closely at the beginning head and body shapes. Using ovals and lines, sketch these.

2 Using curved lines, draw the triangle shape to begin his hood. Add small circles for eyes. Draw curved lines for eyebrows and nose bridge. Lightly sketch the ovals (joints) and lines (rods) to begin his arm and hand.

3 Look at the curved lines that shape his head and face. Add these. Look at the body lines that shape his hood, arm with hanging sleeve, and hand. Draw these. Add four lines to begin his baggy pants.

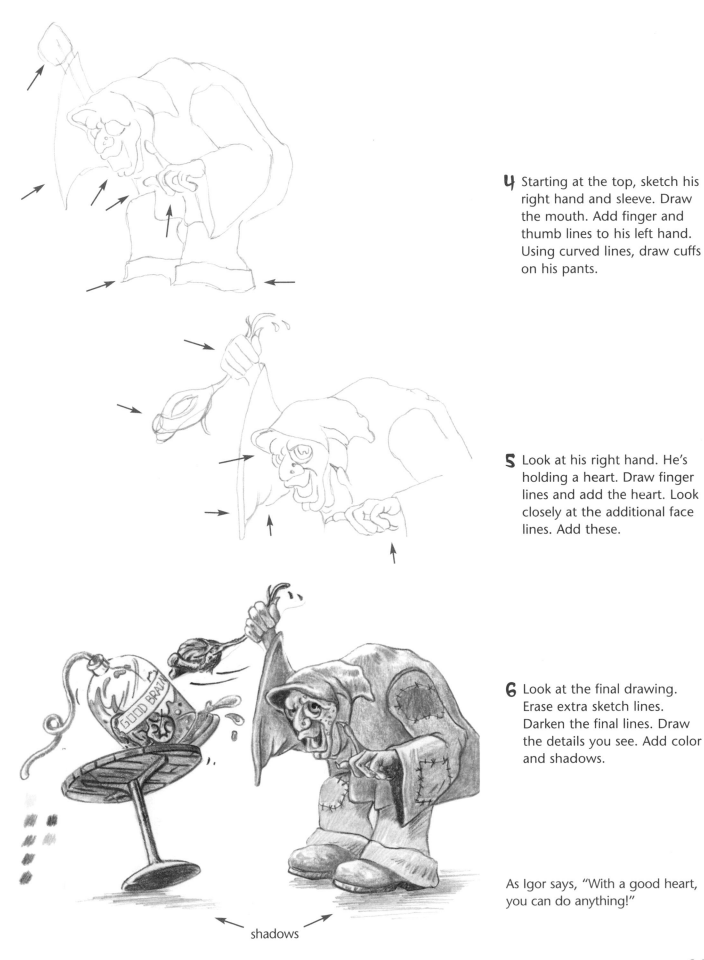

4 Starting at the top, sketch his right hand and sleeve. Draw the mouth. Add finger and thumb lines to his left hand. Using curved lines, draw cuffs on his pants.

5 Look at his right hand. He's holding a heart. Draw finger lines and add the heart. Look closely at the additional face lines. Add these.

6 Look at the final drawing. Erase extra sketch lines. Darken the final lines. Draw the details you see. Add color and shadows.

As Igor says, "With a good heart, you can do anything!"

GOOD BRAIN

shadows

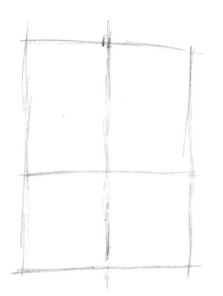
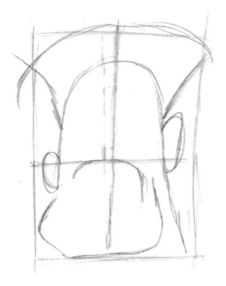

Faces

These step-by-step drawings, across pages 12 and 13, show you how to build interesting faces using basic shapes and lines. Look closely at the shapes, then draw the lines you see.

Remember, your finished drawing doesn't have to look exactly like the illustration shown. Let your imagination go wild. What if the wolf's face had snakeskin instead of fur?

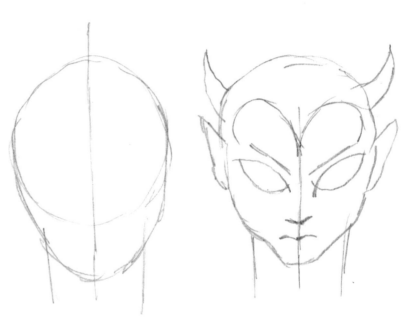

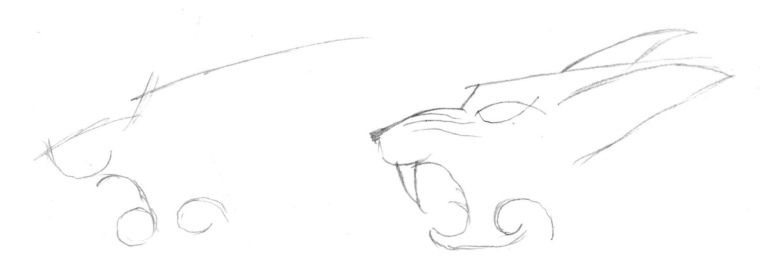

Try drawing Itsy Bitsy,
one itsy bit at a time.

Spare Parts

Frankie is not made of snips and snails, and puppy dog tails. He's stitched together from the remains of others. He has a used liver, another's heart, and leftover brains! I hope it wasn't the one from page 9.

1   Look closely at the angle of the arrows on the clock face. Note the angle of the shapes in the first drawing. Sketch the head shape and lines you see.

2   Starting at the top, draw lines for the hair, nose, and mouth. Add a vest with a V-shaped neckline.

3   Erase the head sketch lines. Add more hair lines. Look closely at the ears, eyes, mouth, and jaw lines. Draw these. Using ovals and curved lines, sketch his left arm. Look at the lines and shapes forming his right arm. Add these.

4   Look closely at the way his fingers wrap around the fence slats. Draw finger lines. Add straight lines for fencing and hinges.

hinge

5 Starting at the top, add stitches and cheekbones. Draw a small oval on his neck to begin his bolt. Using short, squiggly lines, make the vest look shaggy. Add a few curvy lines for his tattered sleeve. Sketch lines (rods) and oval (joints) to begin his leg and boot.

6 Look at the details in the final drawing. Add these. Erase extra sketch lines. Darken the final lines. Add color.

Quickly, rise from your drawing table and lock the door. He's coming through your gate.

Ahhh! Must be the new gardener. Is he here to plant marigolds?

Artist's note: Be creative. Use any colors you want. Green skin? But, of course.

Frankie's Bride

This girl is not made of sugar and spice, and everything nice!

1 Sketch an oval for her head. Add a curved neck line. Sketch a rectangular shape for her hairdo.

2 Look at the shape of her flowing top. Using curved lines, draw it.

3 Look at the position of her raised arms and hands. Sketch ovals (joints) and lines (rods) to begin these. Draw curved lines to begin her flipped up hair. Add her mouth. Add lines for the folds on her top. Add a V-shaped waist line.

4 Look closely at the arms and fingers. Using curved lines, draw these. Add more hair lines. Draw her eyebrow, eye, and nose. Sketch ovals (joints) and lines (rods) to begin her legs and feet. Draw lines to shape these.

5 Starting at the top, draw finger lines. Add squiggly lines for the white middle section of her hair. Add an eyeball. Draw more hair lines. Look closely at her tattered gown. Draw it. Erase extra sketch lines.

6 Look at the details in the final drawing. Add the crumbling roses in her left hand and other details you see. Darken the final lines. Add color.

As Frankie says, "What a bride!"

Dracula

Late at night when all are sleeping, that's the time ole' Drac goes creeping. That's the time he goes searching for something to quench his thirst.

1 Lightly sketch the curved guidelines to begin Dracula's head and cowl.

2 Look closely at the shape of his head profile and draw it overlapping the guidelines. Add spiked hair, a horn, and a pointed ear. Using curved lines, draw the shoulder cape Add ties under his chin. Erase extra sketch lines.

3 Look closely at his raised right arm and hand. Using curved lines, draw it and the sweeping cape lines on both sides of his body. Look at the angle of his body and left arm. Carefully draw the lines and shapes you see. Sketch ovals (joints) and lines (rods) to begin his legs and feet.

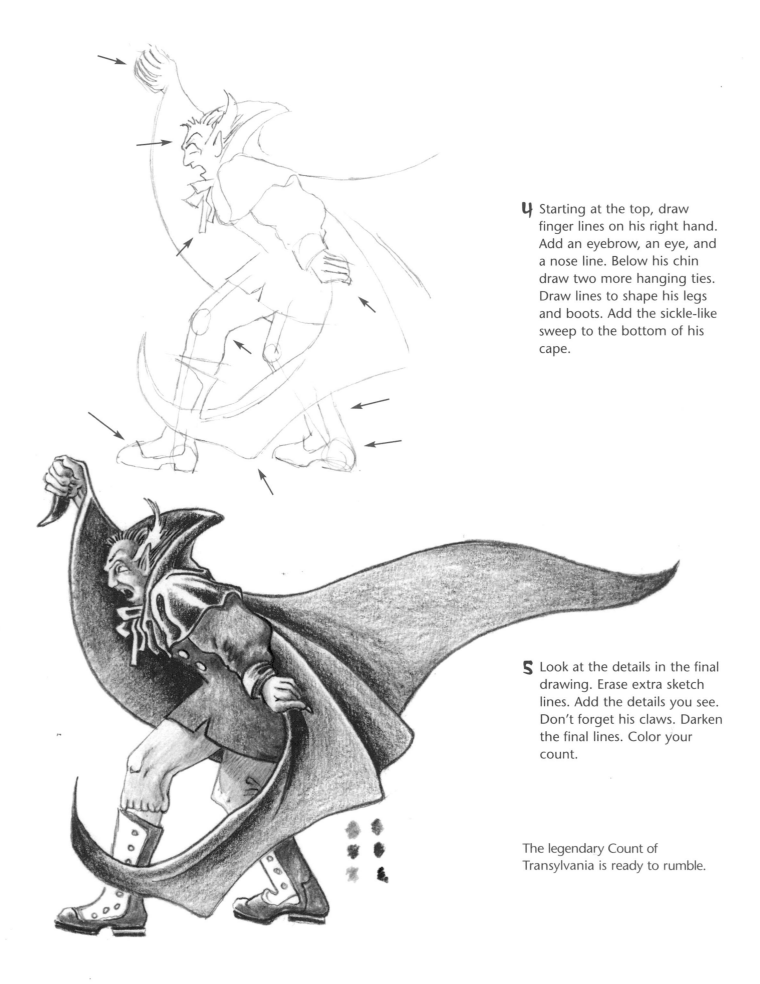

4 Starting at the top, draw finger lines on his right hand. Add an eyebrow, an eye, and a nose line. Below his chin draw two more hanging ties. Draw lines to shape his legs and boots. Add the sickle-like sweep to the bottom of his cape.

5 Look at the details in the final drawing. Erase extra sketch lines. Add the details you see. Don't forget his claws. Darken the final lines. Color your count.

The legendary Count of Transylvania is ready to rumble.

Dracula's Daughter

Daddy was a vampire, mommy was a vampire. Grandpa was a vampire...you get the idea. Dracula's daughter haunts the graveyard with a cold heart and a hot bite.

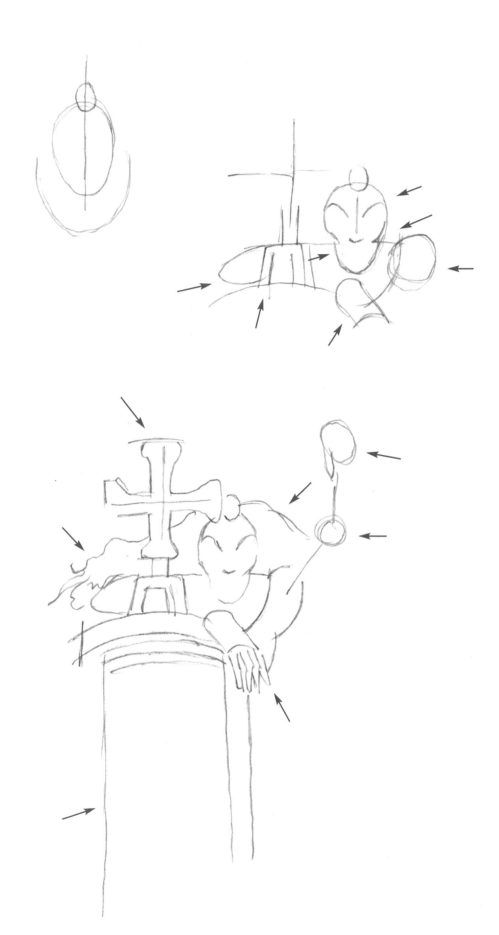

1 Lightly sketch the head ovals and curved neckline. Sketch a guideline down the middle.

2 Look closely at the shapes and lines in the second drawing. Starting at the top of the head oval, add eyebrows, cheek bones, and the tip of her nose. Sketch lines to begin the cross and gravestone. Add arm and shoulder lines.

3 Add curved lines around the cross. Look at her flowing hair. Draw it. Add lines to the gravestone. Draw fingers on her right hand. Add curved body lines under her left shoulder. Using lines (rods) and ovals (joints) sketch the raised left arm and hand.

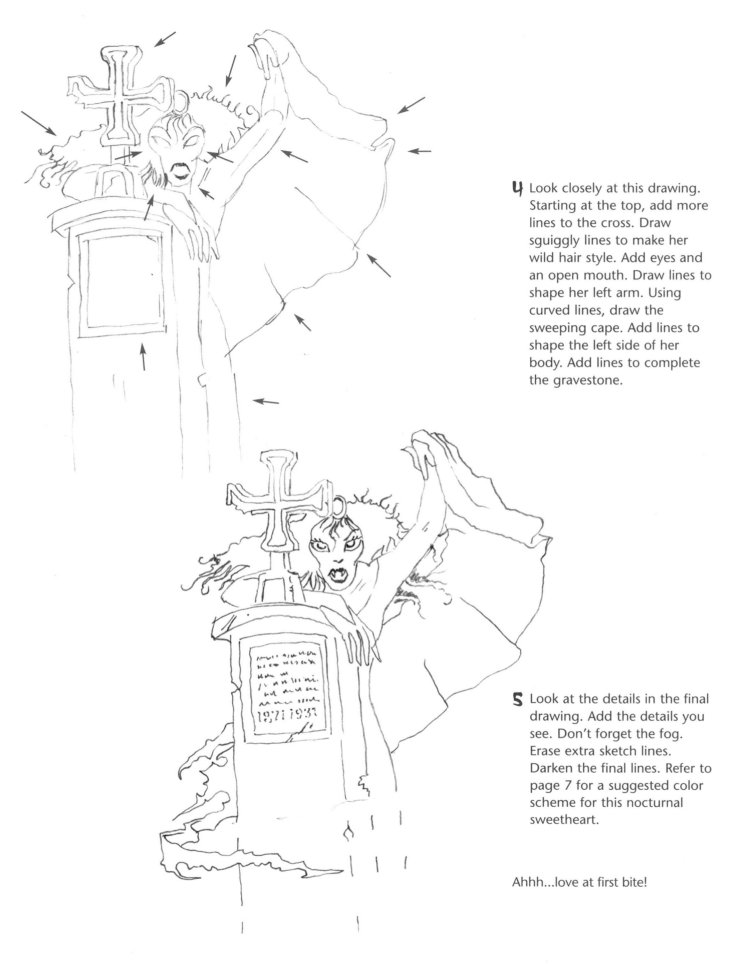

4 Look closely at this drawing. Starting at the top, add more lines to the cross. Draw sguiggly lines to make her wild hair style. Add eyes and an open mouth. Draw lines to shape her left arm. Using curved lines, draw the sweeping cape. Add lines to shape the left side of her body. Add lines to complete the gravestone.

5 Look at the details in the final drawing. Add the details you see. Don't forget the fog. Erase extra sketch lines. Darken the final lines. Refer to page 7 for a suggested color scheme for this nocturnal sweetheart.

Ahhh...love at first bite!

Haunted House

Nothing illustrates better the progression of a drawing from simple to complex like a house or a building.

1 Look closely at the basic shapes in this house. Using lines and simple geometric shapes, lightly sketch the haunted house.

2 Look closely at the details
added in this drawing. See
the dashed lines. These are to
remind you of the sketch lines
used in the first drawing on
page 22.

3 Look at the final drawing. Notice the different textures and patterns. For contrast, some areas are detailed and colored while some are left unfinished.

Use your imagination and the drawing techniques you have learned to finish this drawing. Starting at the top, add the details you see. Don't forget the vampire in the doorway and the skulls. Add shading and color.

Add background if you dare. Perhaps gravestones or creepy, twisted trees. Use your wild imagination!

Happy Haunting!

The Mummy

This guy has been sleeping for quite a while and he doesn't look too happy about being awakened.

1 Look closely at the angle of the arrows on the clock face. Notice the angle of the keyhole shape. Lightly sketch the lines that form it.

2 Look again. Add the additional lines and oval to begin his Egyptian headdress.

3 Look at the shapes that begin his upper body. Using curved and straight lines, sketch these. Add a curved line near the middle to form his chin.

4 Using ovals and curved lines, draw the biceps, forearm, and right hand. Add a squiggly line to begin his big (foreshortened) left hand. Sketch the lines (rods) and oval (joints) to begin the legs.

Artist's tip: Foreshortening is used in perspective drawings to show the lines of an object shorter than they are in order to give the illusion of proper relative size.

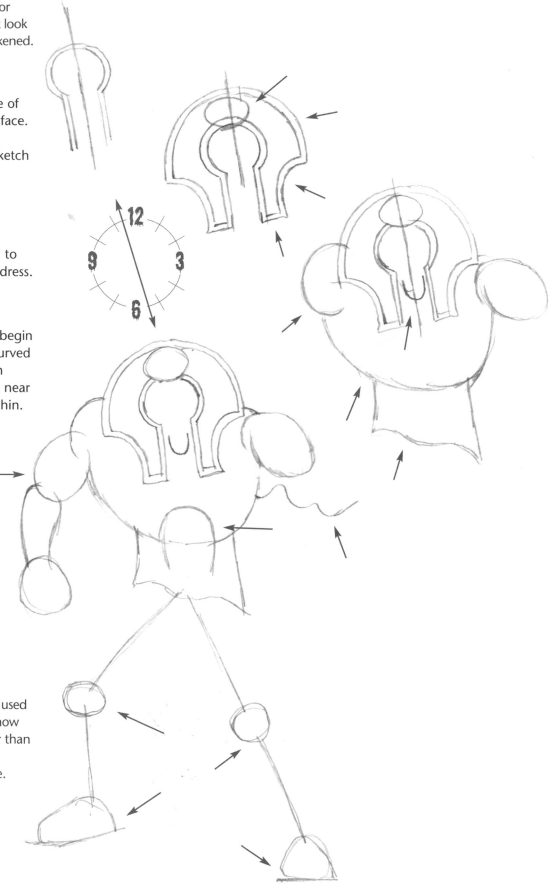

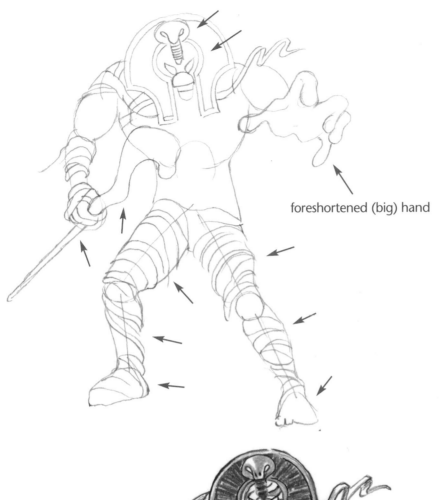

foreshortened (big) hand

5 Look closely, head to toe, at the details in this drawing. Starting at the top, add the the cobra headpiece. Draw the eyes, nose, and mouth. Using curved lines, finish drawing his arms and hands. Add the cobra staff. Look at the angle of his legs. Draw his legs and feet.

6 Look at the final drawing. Erase extra sketch lines. Darken the final lines. Add color and a shadow.

Did you call out "Mommy" or "Mummy?" Hmm...maybe it's time to move along....

Cuddly Witch

Where would great stories like Hansel and Gretel or The Wizard of Oz be with out the wicked witch? Instead of a really wicked one, let's make a cuddly witch.

1 Look at the beginning head shape. Using curved lines, sketch it.

2 Look closely at the shapes that form the hat. Sketch these. Add the triangle shaped ears. Using curved lines, draw the hat brim and begin the arms.

3 Add eyes and a thin mouth. Draw an oval for the cat's head. Sketch lines for arms and hand shapes.

4 Look closely at the shapes emerging. Starting at the top, draw the owl shape. Add an eyeball and a gnarly nose. Draw the cat's ears. Using curved lines, add her long fingers. Draw the big belly line. Using straight and curved lines, draw a staff in her right hand. Add the cat's tail. Sketch straight lines for legs and feet.

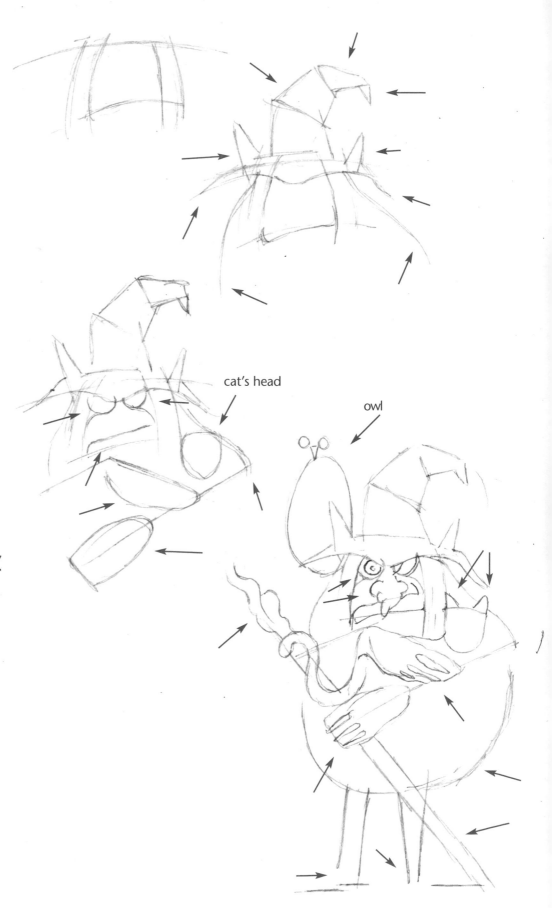

cat's head

owl

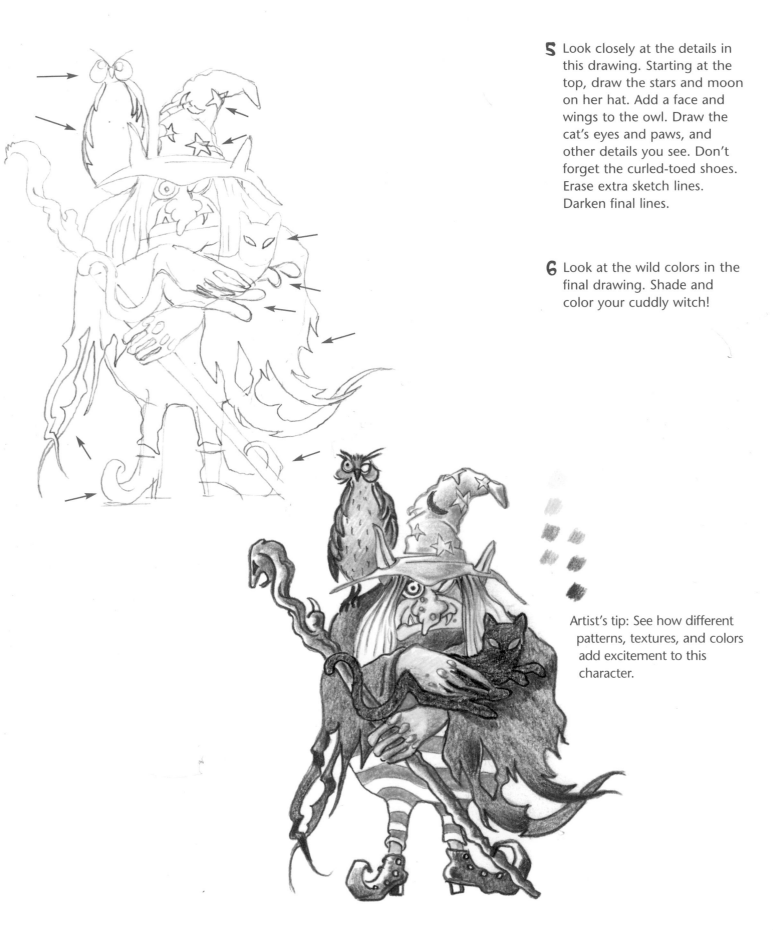

5 Look closely at the details in this drawing. Starting at the top, draw the stars and moon on her hat. Add a face and wings to the owl. Draw the cat's eyes and paws, and other details you see. Don't forget the curled-toed shoes. Erase extra sketch lines. Darken final lines.

6 Look at the wild colors in the final drawing. Shade and color your cuddly witch!

Artist's tip: See how different patterns, textures, and colors add excitement to this character.

Devil or Angel?

1 First, look at the clock face to determine the angle of Beelzebub's head. Look closely at the shapes that begin the head and upper body. Sketch these.

2 Using curved lines, draw his chest. Add long curved lines for abdominal muscles.

3 Draw his big, open, asymmetrical mouth. Look at the ovals and curved lines that form the shoulders and upper arms. Sketch these. Draw the outline of his muscular torso.

4 Starting at the top, sketch a line and rectangle to begin his right arm. Look at his facial expression. Add these lines. Using curved lines, divide his abdominals into eight sections. Draw his left hand and finger.

Artist's tip: Asymmetric (or asymmetrical) means unbalanced. The two sides of his mouth are not the same.

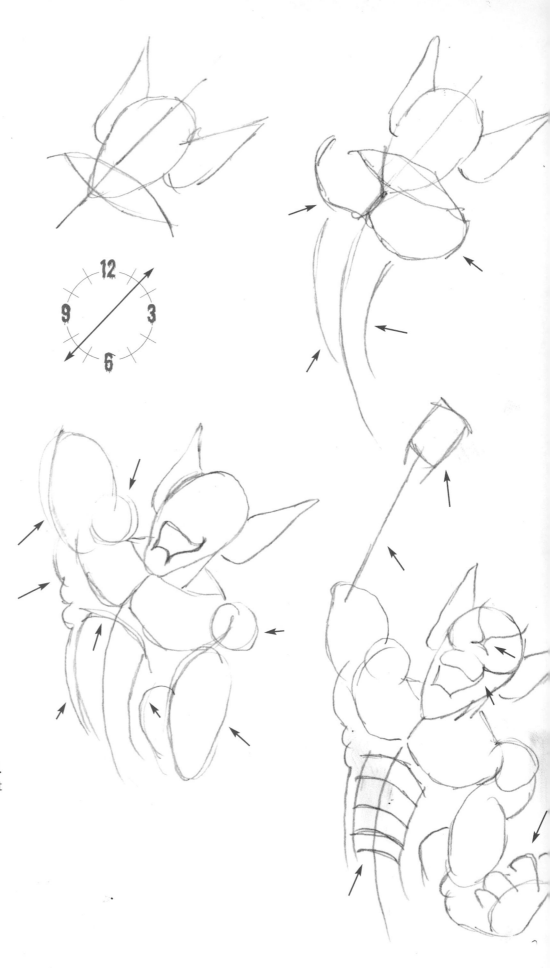

30   DRAW MONSTERS

5 Look at the shape and thickness of his right arm and hand. Draw these. Using straight and curved lines, draw the spear. Add eyebrows, a nose, and hair on the pointed chin. Draw spikes on the shoulders. Look closely at his abdominal muscles, curled left hand, and flames shooting up from below. (Where else?) Erase extra sketch lines. Darken the final lines.

6 Look at the final drawing. Add the details you see. Don't forget his fangs, horns, and pitchfork. Shade and color your fallen angel.

Artist's tip: Sketch lightly until the final stages of your drawing. Avoid drawing small sketches. Keep your drawings at least the size of the ones in this book.

3-D lettering

Combining block letters and perspective you can create awesome lettering for signs or gravestones. Begin with simple block letters. Add flat pencil shading, as in letters Y and O for depth. Or, create realism with more details and more shading, as in letters N and D.

Use block letters once again to create the word SCARY. This time, be even more creative. Add more details, textures, and shading. Let your imagination run wild.

Try drawing different type styles. Have fun! Use your imagination!

Anatomy lesson

By knowing how bones fit together, their approximate size, and their relationship to each other, you can draw a more realistic monster. Skull to toe, look closely at the bone structure of this one.

1. skull

2. clavicle

3. scapula

4. humerus

5. ulna

6. radius

7. carpals

8. metacarpals

9. phalanges

10. sternum

11. rib cage

12. spinal column

13. pelvis

14. femur

15. patella

16. tibia

17. fibula

18. tarsals

19. metatarsals

20. phalanges

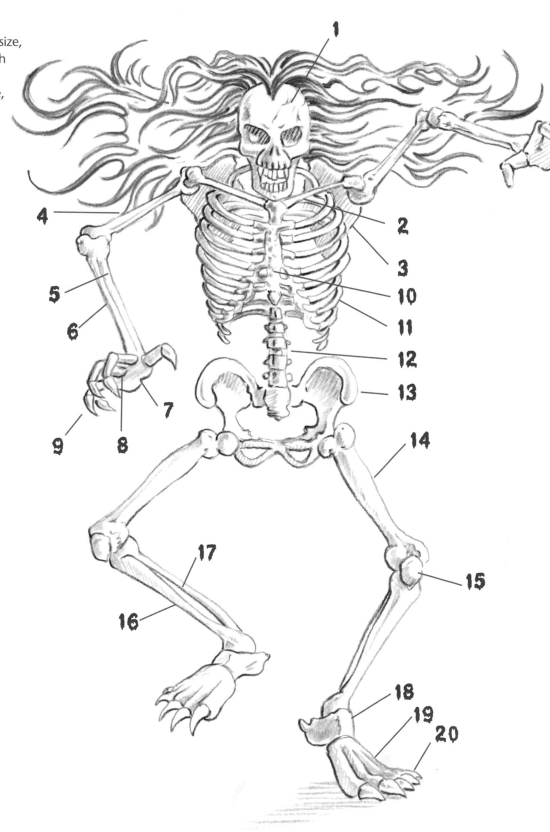

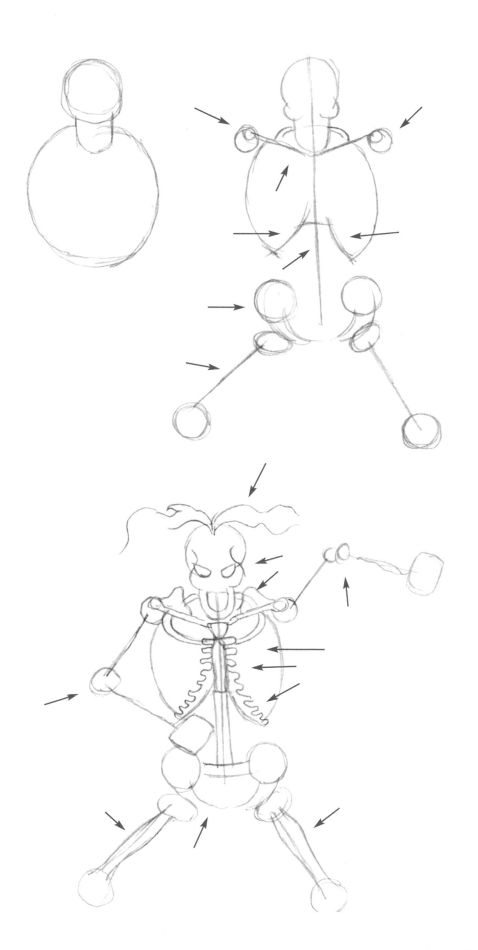

Did you notice the symmetry of the skeleton? Let's draw one.

1 Look closely at the shapes that begin the skull and upper body. Lightly sketch these.

2 Sketch a long, V-shaped line under the jaw, with a circle at each end to begin the shoulders. Look closely at the lines that form the rib cage. Draw these. Using lines (rods) and ovals (joints), sketch the lower body and thigh bones.

3 Starting at the top, add a few curvy lines for hair. Draw eye sockets and a mouth. Look again at the bone structure of the arms and upper body. Sketch the lines and shapes you see. Draw the rib cage cartilage (kind of like a zipper being unzipped). Add back bone lines and the femur bone lines.

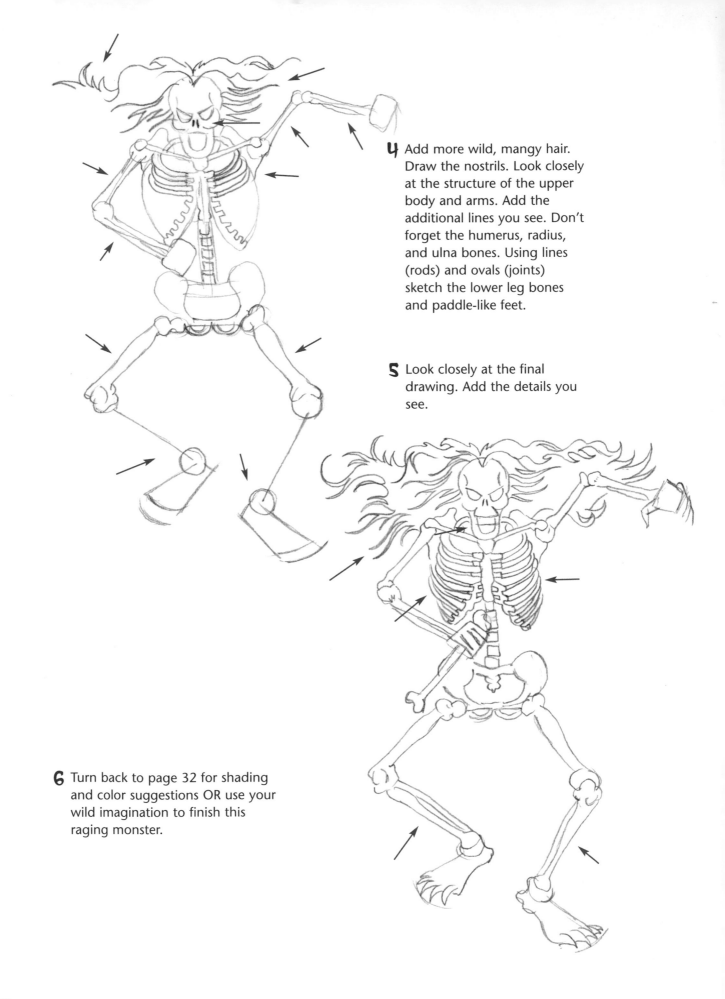

4 Add more wild, mangy hair. Draw the nostrils. Look closely at the structure of the upper body and arms. Add the additional lines you see. Don't forget the humerus, radius, and ulna bones. Using lines (rods) and ovals (joints) sketch the lower leg bones and paddle-like feet.

5 Look closely at the final drawing. Add the details you see.

6 Turn back to page 32 for shading and color suggestions OR use your wild imagination to finish this raging monster.

Swamp Monster

Way back along the Bayou where the bullfrogs croak and the gators feed, on ominous slimy green things, the swamp monster waits patiently for his next meal. He prefers the two-legged variety, but doesn't mind a little lizard snack. So, if you've got a lizard in your pocket, that might buy you a minute or so....

1 Look at the angle of the arrows on the clock face. Look at the angle and the shapes of the head and shoulders. Sketch the shapes you see.

2 Look at the head fins. Sketch these and two ovals for his left arm. Sketch a straight line for his left side.

3 Add spines to his head fins. Draw eyes, eyebrows, and a mouth line. Look at the lines and shapes that begin his right arm, legs, and tail. Sketch these.

4 Starting at the top, draw jagged lines over the head and fin sketch lines. Add more spine lines. Go over and darken the body and tail lines. Erase extra sketch lines. Look at the shapes of the hands and feet. Draw the shapes you see.

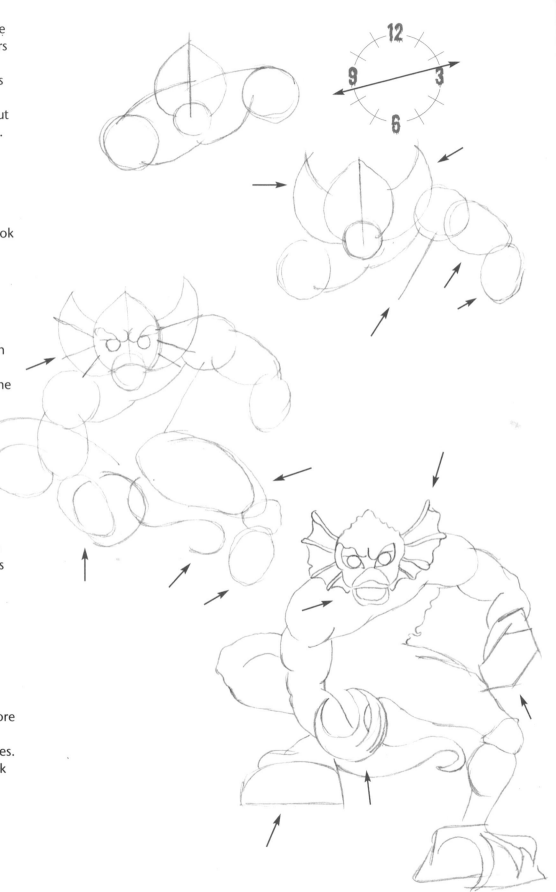

5 Look closely at the details in this drawing. See the dripping lines and hanging ooze. Starting at the top, add the details you see.

6 Turn back to page 37 to get ideas for shading and coloring your Swamp Monster. Take a closer look at background details. What other details could you add to create a more ominous scene? Add additional details. Shade and color your drawing.

(You know, on second thought, forget the lizard. You've probably got room for a fairly good-sized iguana in your backpack.)

Scorpio

Ray Harryhausen was one of Hollywood's premier special effects wizards. He created tingles and screams on the big screen with his stop action Medusa in The Clash of the Titans. Let's draw a Scorpio as part human, part insect, and part mechanical, like many of Harry's great creations.

1 Look at the angle of the arrows on the clock face. Notice the angle of the head oval in the beginning sketch. Using ovals and curved lines, sketch the shapes you see.

2 Look at the human-like body emerging. Using ovals and curved lines, sketch these shapes.

3 Look closely at the insect parts emerging. Draw curved lines on top to begin the tail. Add abdominal lines. Draw curved lines for hips. Look at the shapes forming the big claw and pinchers. Draw these.

4 Starting at the top, add curved lines to thicken the tail. Look at the extending right arm and hand shapes. Draw these. Look closely at the shape of his left arm/claw with pinchers. Add the details you see. Sketch the two front legs shapes.

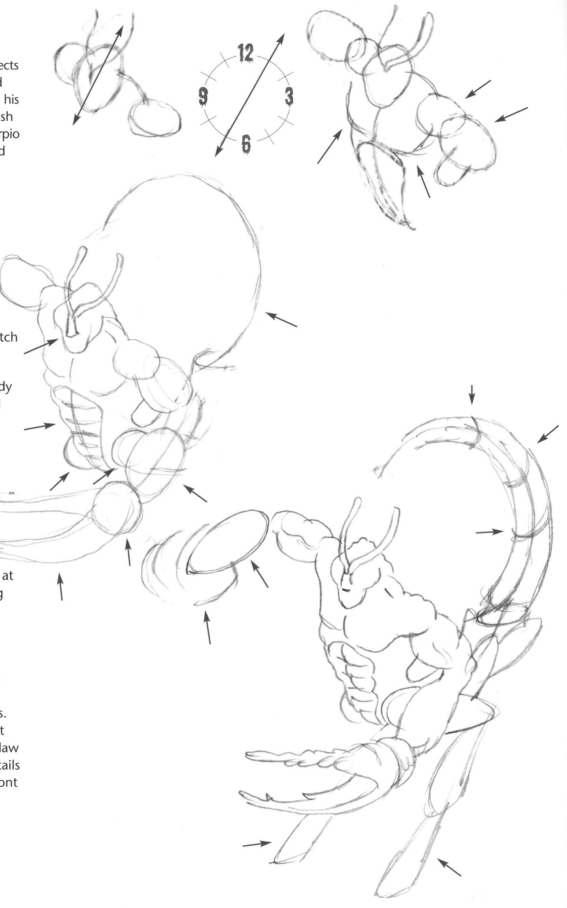

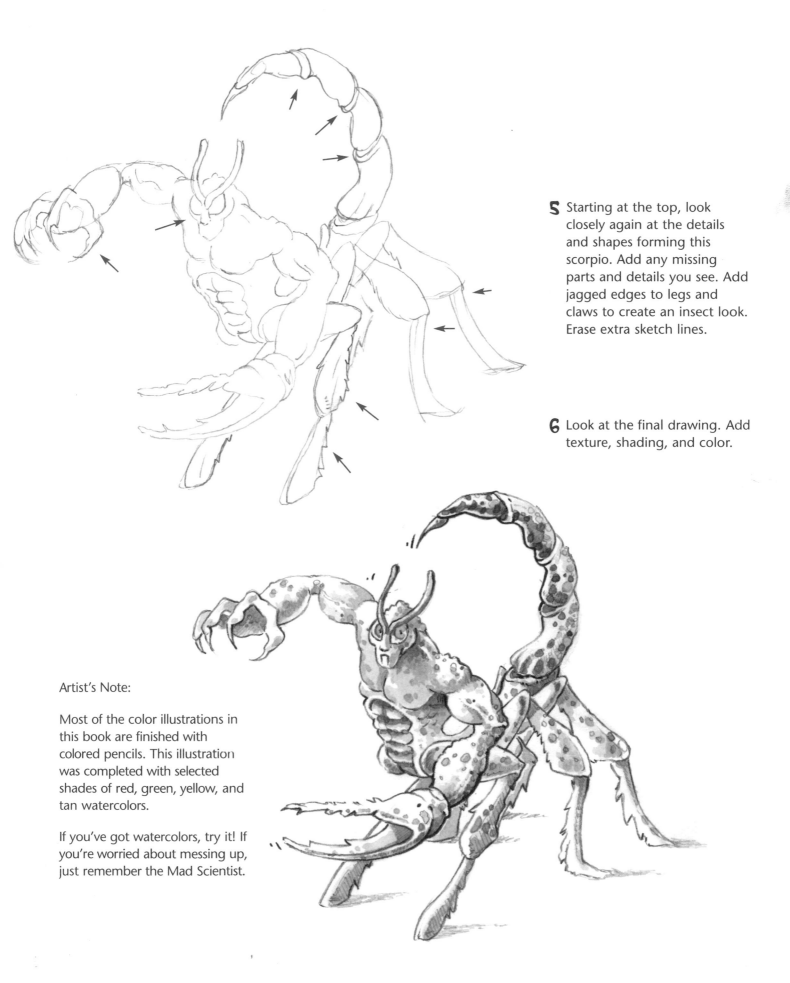

5 Starting at the top, look closely again at the details and shapes forming this scorpio. Add any missing parts and details you see. Add jagged edges to legs and claws to create an insect look. Erase extra sketch lines.

6 Look at the final drawing. Add texture, shading, and color.

Artist's Note:

Most of the color illustrations in this book are finished with colored pencils. This illustration was completed with selected shades of red, green, yellow, and tan watercolors.

If you've got watercolors, try it! If you're worried about messing up, just remember the Mad Scientist.

Werewolf

Usually the result of an evil curse, the werewolf is a human being who changes into a wolf. This one is changing rapidly. Better sketch him fast before he starts howling at the moon.

1 Look closely at the oval and curved lines shaping the werewolf's torso. Lightly sketch the shapes you see.

2 Now look at the different lines and shapes that form the head outline. Sketch these.

3 Starting at the top, draw the shaggy mane, pointed ears, eyebrows, and facial features. Erase extra head guidelines. Sketch lines (rods) and an oval (joints) to begin his right arm. Draw pectoral and chest lines. Look closely at the shapes and angles of his legs and feet. Sketch these. Add lines to begin his torn pants.

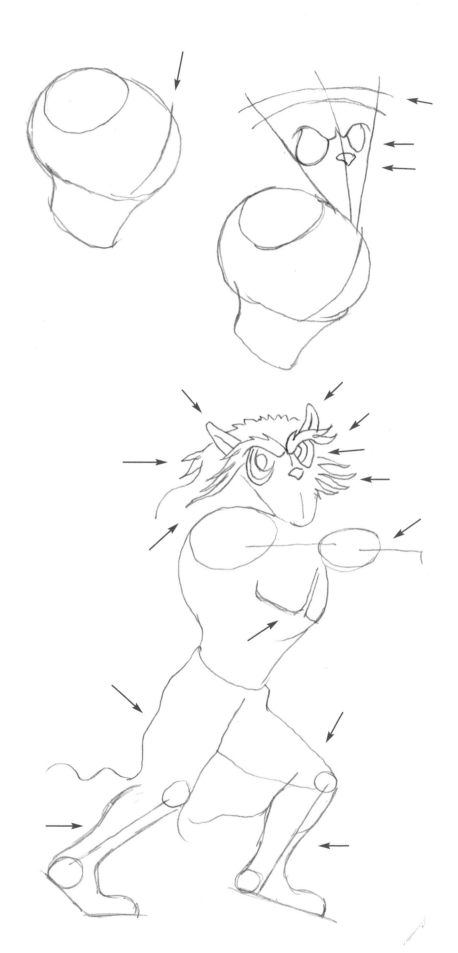

4 Look closely, head to toe, and add all the details you see.

5 Look at the final drawing. Add short pencil strokes for texture. Add additional details you see. Shade and color.

STAND BACK!!!

Wow! What a werewolf!

Looks like he's ready to boogie on.

Gator woman

Half gator, half human, this gator woman escaped from some carnival sideshow. She now hangs out just below the surface of a favorite swimming hole. You might want to avoid the murky waters of that ole' swimmin' hole, especially at night!

1 Look at the ovals and curved lines that begin this creature. Lightly sketch the head and body shapes.

2 Draw a long curved eyebrow line and a curved line to begin the ear. Add the long wavy tail.

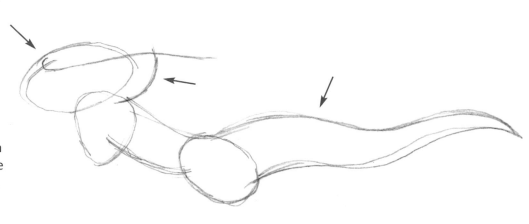

3 Look closely at the angles in this drawing. Starting at the top, add the zigzag scales on her back and tail. Draw a line along the bottom of the tail. Look at the lines (rods) and ovals (joints) that form her arms and legs. Sketch these. Draw paw-like hands and claw-like feet.

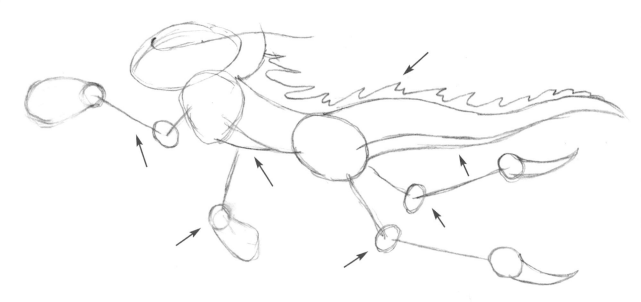

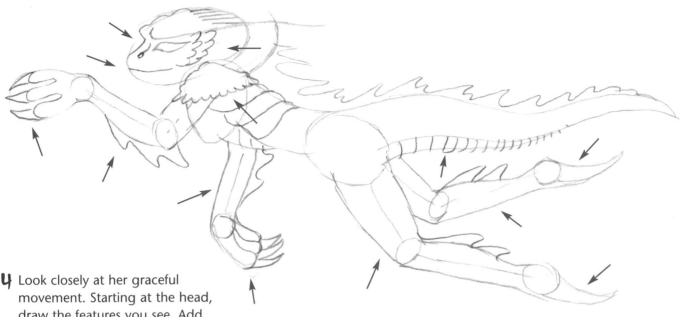

4 Look closely at her graceful movement. Starting at the head, draw the features you see. Add scales on her shoulder and lines on her side. Add lines under her tail. Look closely at the details on her arms and legs. Using curved lines, draw these.

5 Look at the final drawing. Erase extra sketch lines. Draw all the details you see. Darken final lines. Add texture with small circles for scales. Shade and color to enhance her gator look.

GREAT gator!

Lighting

When adding texture, final lines, shading, or color it is important to know the direction of the light source.

In all three of these drawings, the light is coming from the left side of the page.

Draw these, keeping the direction of the light in mind.

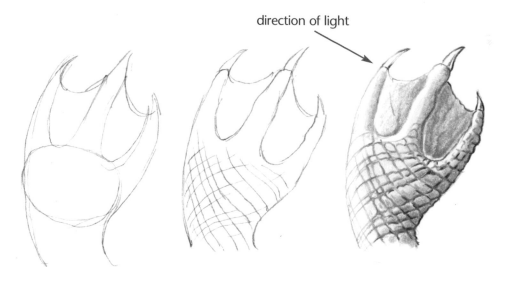

direction of light

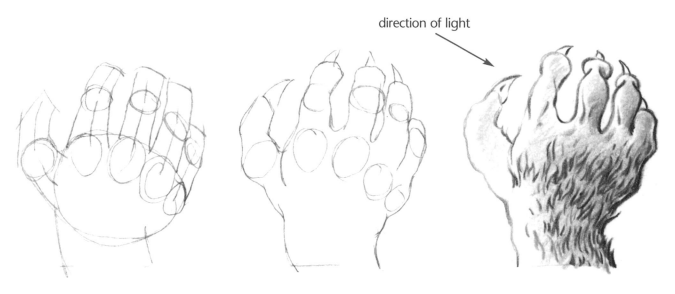

direction of light

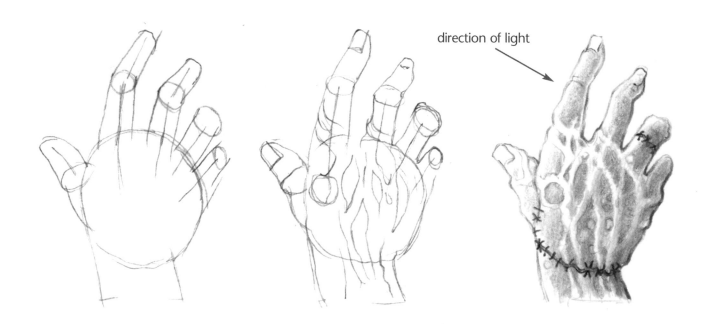

direction of light

Earl E. Riser

In the wee morning hours when all we mortals sleep, that's the time the undead stir. That's the time they creep and claw their way to freedom from their decomposing graves. Sunrise to sunset, the same old grind, day after day.

1 Look at the angle of the arrows on the clock face. Look at the angle and shape of Earl's head. Sketch the circle and lines to begin his head.

2 Sketch the ovals and curved line to begin his shoulders.

3 Sketch the lines and ovals to begin his arms. Draw a squiggly line above his left arm to begin the grave pit. Add ears, eyebrows, a nose, and a chin.

4 Look closely at the emerging shapes. Starting at the top, add the lines and shapes you see.

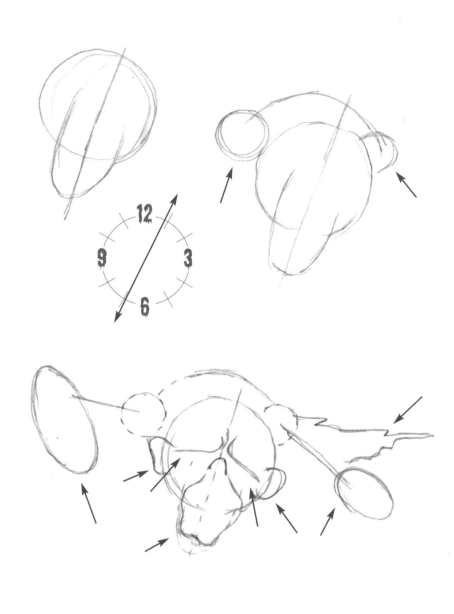

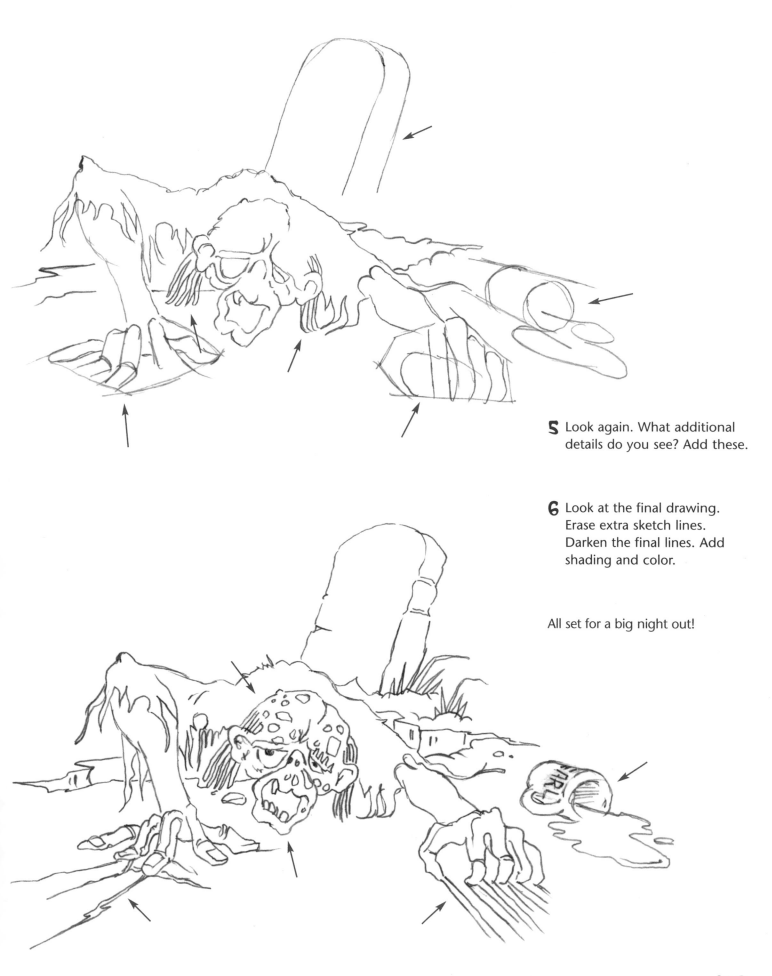

5 Look again. What additional details do you see? Add these.

6 Look at the final drawing. Erase extra sketch lines. Darken the final lines. Add shading and color.

All set for a big night out!

Prom Queen

This Prom Queen has been hanging around a long time just waiting for Mr. Right!

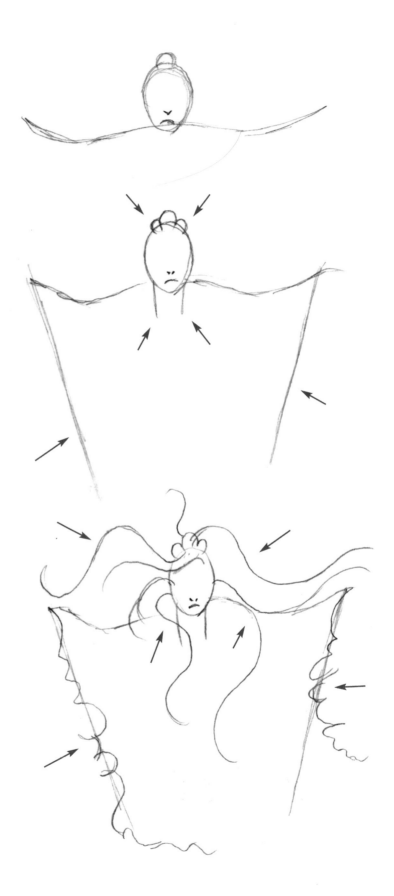

1 Look at the first drawing. Draw the head and extended arm lines you see.

2 Starting at the top, add the curved hair lines you see. Draw two neck lines. Add a diagonal line down from each arm.

3 Look closely, head to toe. Add all the details you see.

4 Add even more hair to this ghastly beauty. Draw her hollow eyes and eyebrows. Add arms and hands. Draw her flowing gown. Add her feet.

5 Look at the final drawing. Add Add the details you see. Shade and add color.

Care to dance?

Zombie

Zombies here! Zombies there!
Walking corpses everywhere!

1 Look at the first drawing.
Sketch his oddly-shaped skull.

2 Sketch two circles below the
skull for the shoulder and hip
joint.

3 Look closely at the shapes and
lines forming the zombie's
body. Add eyes. Draw his arm
and hand. Add lines to form
his torso. Sketch light lines to
show the direction of his legs.
Add leg lines and boot lines.

4 Draw dreadlocks. Add his
second arm and finger lines
on his right hand. Draw coat
lines. Add boot lines.

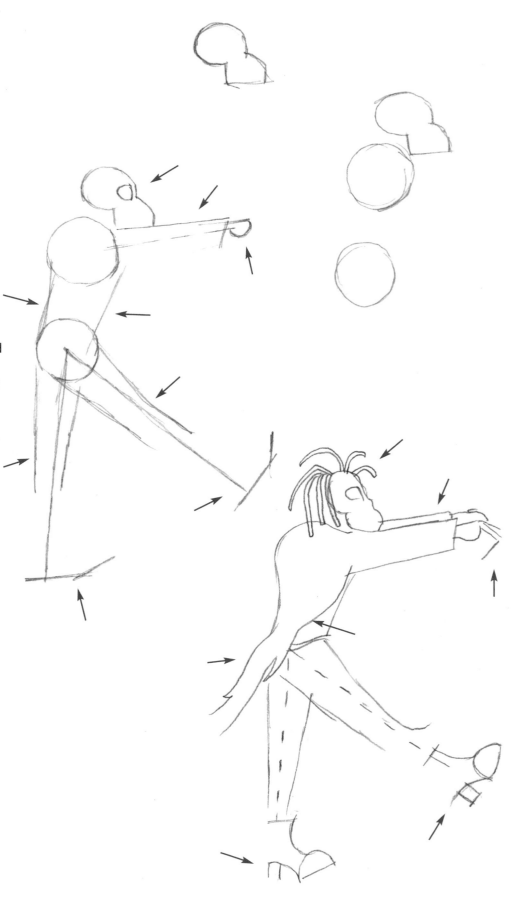

5 Look closely at the details in this drawing. Add the details you see. Erase extra sketch lines.

6 Look at the final drawing. Add more details. Shade and color your zombie.

This guy's got style. Perhaps he'd like to dance with the Prom Queen.

Bed Bug

You know that pesky little itch you feel at the back of your leg right before you fall asleep at night? Yeah, that one. The one that's just annoying enough to keep you awake. Perhaps it's this little guy with his set of lobster-like pinchers having a party at your expense.

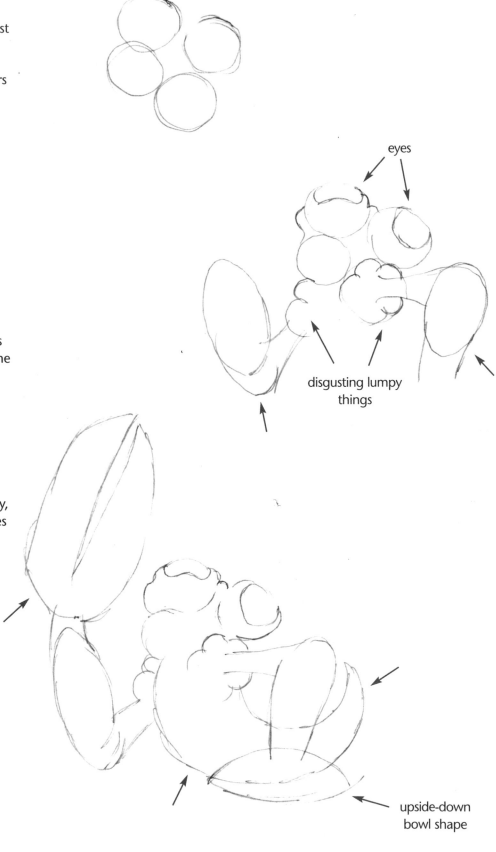

1 Sketch four circles close together to begin this pesky critter.

2 Look closely at the shapes emerging. Sketch the shapes and lines you see to begin the head and body.

eyes

disgusting lumpy things

3 Look again at the arms, body, and tail lines. Sketch the lines and shapes you see.

upside-down bowl shape

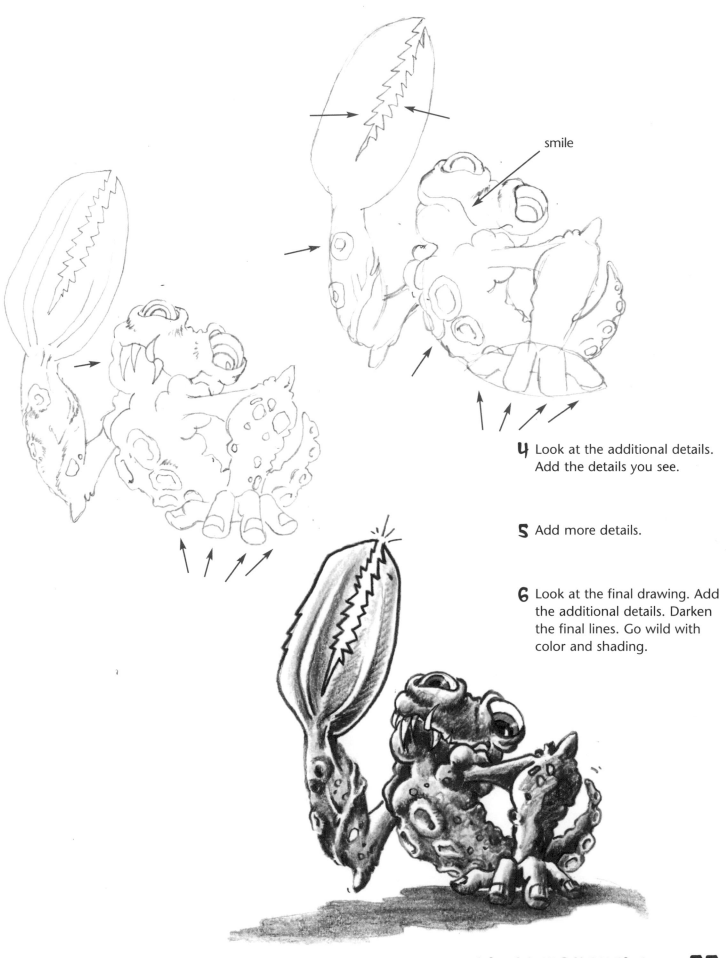

smile

4 Look at the additional details. Add the details you see.

5 Add more details.

6 Look at the final drawing. Add the additional details. Darken the final lines. Go wild with color and shading.

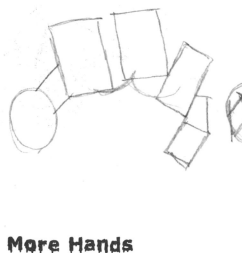

More Hands

The first hand begins as lines (rods) and shapes (joints). See how easily you can start with simple lines and shapes.

The next hand emphasizes the use of shapes for hand and finger construction. It also emphasizes foreshortening (the illusion of reaching forward). By making parts of the hand larger, the artist creates depth and perspective.

Try your hand at drawing these.

Toxic man

Somewhere deep in mother earth's crust, toxic ooze and industrial sludge bubble up.

1 Look at the angle of the arrows on the clock face. Sketch the head oval at the same angle. Add a line to begin the body.

2 Add curved lines to begin shoulders and chest.

3 Look closely at the shapes emerging in this drawing. Starting at the top, add the shapes and lines you see.

4 Sketch the lines and shapes extending his right and left arms and hands. Draw his eye and nose. Look closely at the dripping sludge puddle. Draw it.

anguished mouth

bulging pecs

action lines

5 Look closely at the details and color added in this drawing. Add the details and color you see. Erase extra sketch lines.

6 Look at the final drawing. Add more details. Shade and color. Don't get too close or he just might slime you.

Aside from the slime, he's got a certain charm, no?

Dungeon Master

This guy keeps the castle prisoners in line. He's a likable enough fellow when he's home with the wife and kids but heaven help you if you're shackled to his dungeon wall.

1 Look at the shape and lines that begin his head and shoulders. Sketch these.

2 Draw lines to begin his curling horns and the two small horns on top. Add his drooping ears. Draw two curved lines for his chest.

3 Add his nose and eyes. Look at the oval shapes that begin his arms. Sketch these. Using curved lines, draw the waist and belly.

4 Look closely, top to bottom. Add the details you see. Don't forget his goat-like hooves.

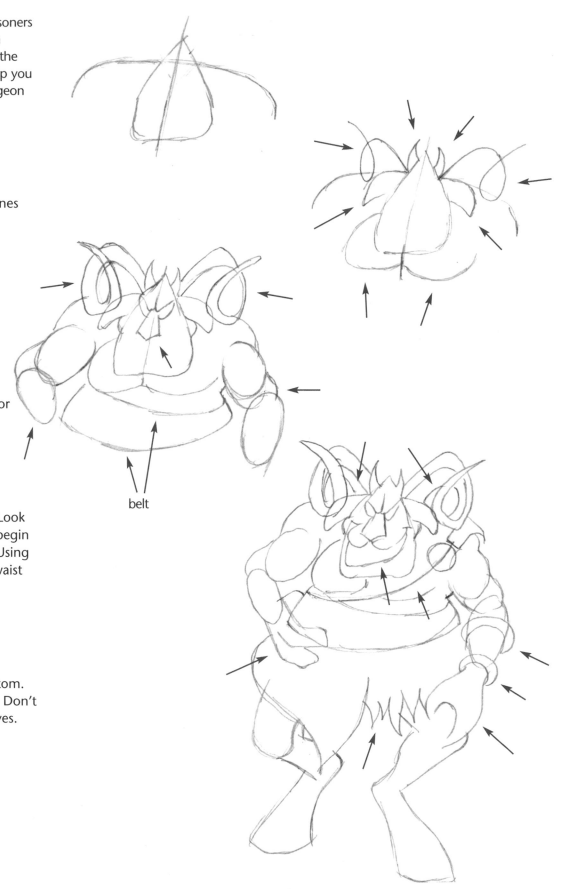

belt

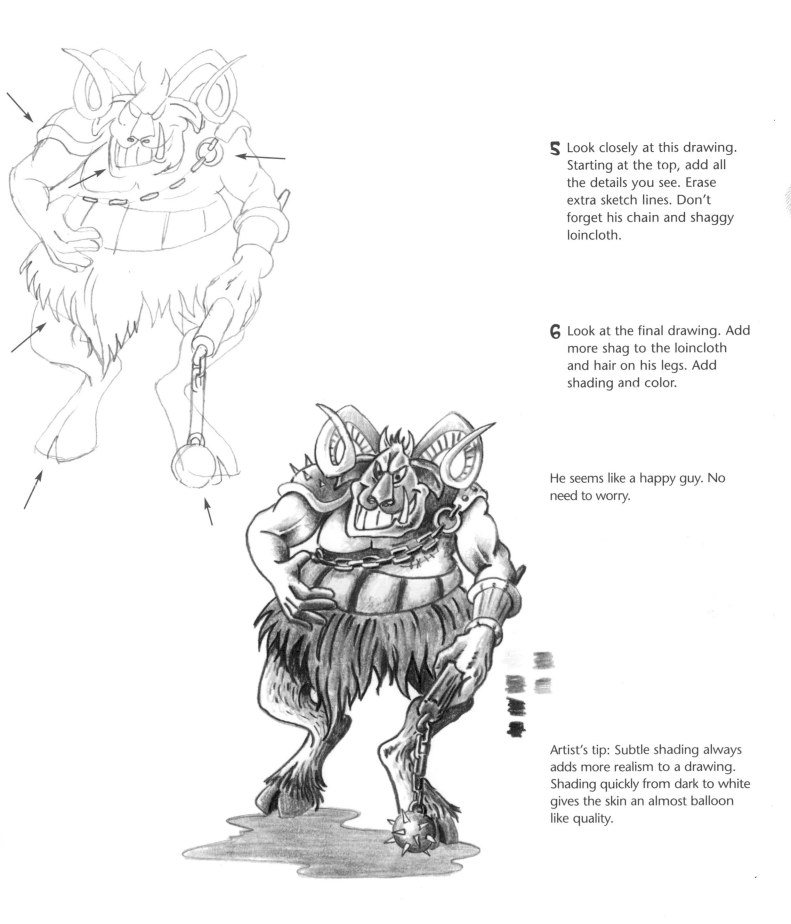

5 Look closely at this drawing. Starting at the top, add all the details you see. Erase extra sketch lines. Don't forget his chain and shaggy loincloth.

6 Look at the final drawing. Add more shag to the loincloth and hair on his legs. Add shading and color.

He seems like a happy guy. No need to worry.

Artist's tip: Subtle shading always adds more realism to a drawing. Shading quickly from dark to white gives the skin an almost balloon like quality.

Gargoyle

For centuries our stony friend here has guarded this old cemetery. After all these years of standing watch, he is finally ready to burst loose and have some fun.

1 Sketch the lines and shapes that form the skull and begin the shoulders.

2 Sketch the oval and lines to shape the torso.

3 Look closely at the angles of the ovals forming his arms. Starting at the top, sketch these. Sketch the circle and half-circle to begin his hips. Draw a line under these.

4 Look at the shape that begins his right hand. Sketch it. Look closely at the shapes and lines that form his legs and feet. Sketch these.

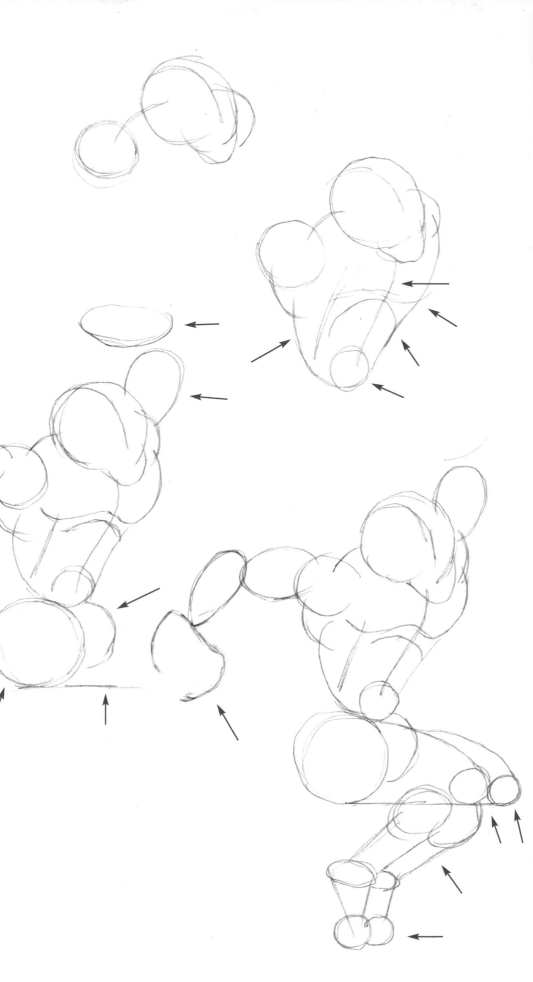

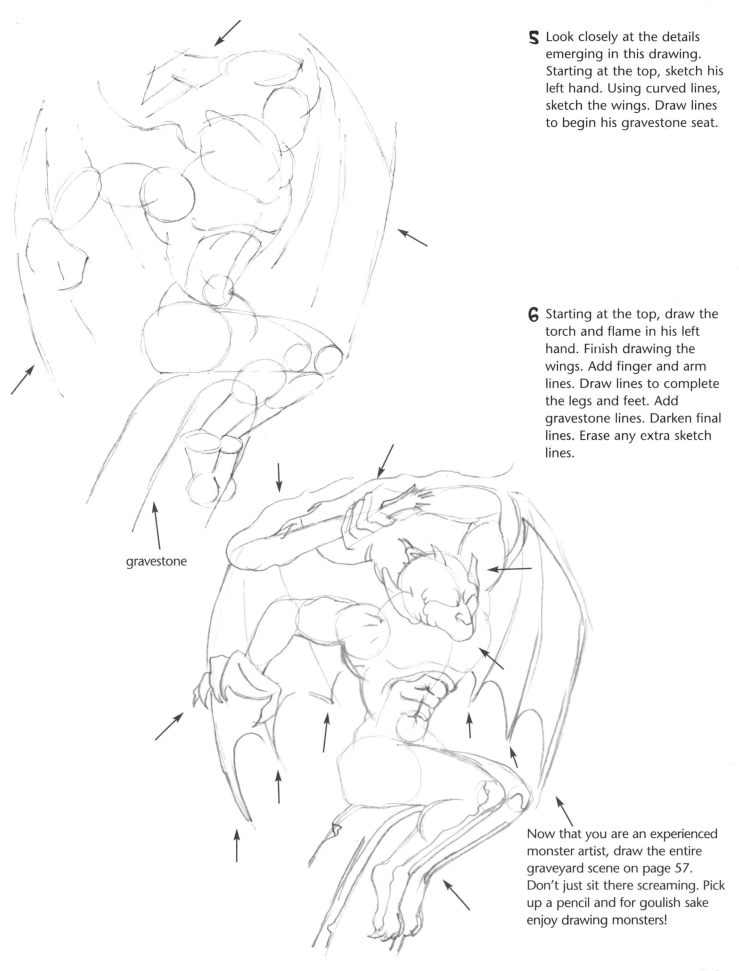

5 Look closely at the details emerging in this drawing. Starting at the top, sketch his left hand. Using curved lines, sketch the wings. Draw lines to begin his gravestone seat.

6 Starting at the top, draw the torch and flame in his left hand. Finish drawing the wings. Add finger and arm lines. Draw lines to complete the legs and feet. Add gravestone lines. Darken final lines. Erase any extra sketch lines.

gravestone

Now that you are an experienced monster artist, draw the entire graveyard scene on page 57. Don't just sit there screaming. Pick up a pencil and for goulish sake enjoy drawing monsters!

We hope you've enjoyed this book!

To see our full line of how-to-draw books, please visit **www.drawbooks.com**, or write us:

Drawbooks
PO Box 546
Columbus, NC 28722-0546